ATTACH

This book belongs to:

official member of the
Be The Change Club

Joined on:

To Jackie Russell, Natalie Russell,
Kimberley Trim and Gareth Brierley

First published in the UK in 2016 by

Ivy Press

210 High Street

Lewes

East Sussex BN7 2NS

United Kingdom

www.ivypress.co.uk

British Library Cataloguing-in-Publication Data
A catalogue record for this book is available from the British Library

ISBN: 978-1-78240-328-9

This book was conceived, designed & produced by

Ivy Press

PUBLISHER   Susan Kelly
CREATIVE DIRECTOR Michael Whitehead
EDITORIAL DIRECTOR Tom Kitch
MANAGING EDITOR   Susie Behar
ART DIRECTORS   Hanri van Wyk and Kim Hankinson
DESIGNER   Joanna Clinch
EDITORIAL ASSISTANT Lucy Menzies
DESIGN ASSISTANT   Emily Hurlock
ILLUSTRATOR   David Broadbent

Printed in China

2 4 8 6 8 10 9 7 5 3 1

BE THE
CHANGE
MAKE iT
HAPPEN

BY
BERNADETTE RUSSELL

Illustrated by
DAVID BROADBENT

How you can make a difference

IVY KIDS

CONGRATULATIONS

Opening this book is the first step towards changing the world. You might not realize it, but you are a hero! You have a lot of power, and like a superhero you can use your power to do something and make things happen on the issues you really care about.

The suggestions in the book will help you spread the word, fundraise for important causes, and make a real difference in your community and worldwide. And most importantly, you'll have loads of fun at the same time!

Your Mission:

So, obviously the world is beautiful, and full of fun things to do... but do you secretly sometimes wish that you could change a few things? Well, guess what? You don't need a magic wand to transform the world, you just need YOU! Plus:

- A sprinkle of enthusiasm
- A big splash of energy
- This Book

You can be the superhero the world has been waiting for (with or without a cape. I wear a cape to do my missions, but that's just me).

So, work through this book and by the end you will have transformed into a fully fledged **Change Champion!**

YES!
You can do it!
You can
BE THE CHANGE
and MAKE IT
HAPPEN!

YOU CAN DO IT!

ANIMAL AWARENESS

You know those posters for missing cats and dogs that you see in parks? Make your own MISSING poster for animals in danger of extinction. For example: 'MISSING MOUNTAIN GORILLA' - only 700 remaining due to shrinking habitat.

Once you've found the animal you want to help, research some organizations that help them and put their website details on your poster so people know where to find out more.

Lighten Up

Persuade the grown-ups in your home to change all the regular light bulbs to energy-saving ones. If they need some encouragement you could tell them this POLLUTION FACT: if every household in the U.S.A. replaced one bulb, that would equal removing 1 MILLION cars from the road.

That'll get them up the ladder! (Reward them with a nice cup of tea and a biscuit.)

SILLY SPORTS DAYS

Get a sports committee together with some friends. Each person chooses a silly sport (such as an egg and spoon race, sack race, skittles or juggling).

Hold your sports day in a local park, charging spectators to raise cash for charity. Make trophies for winners out of card that is painted gold, silver and bronze.

TIP: It's very important that both kids and adults are made to look silly.

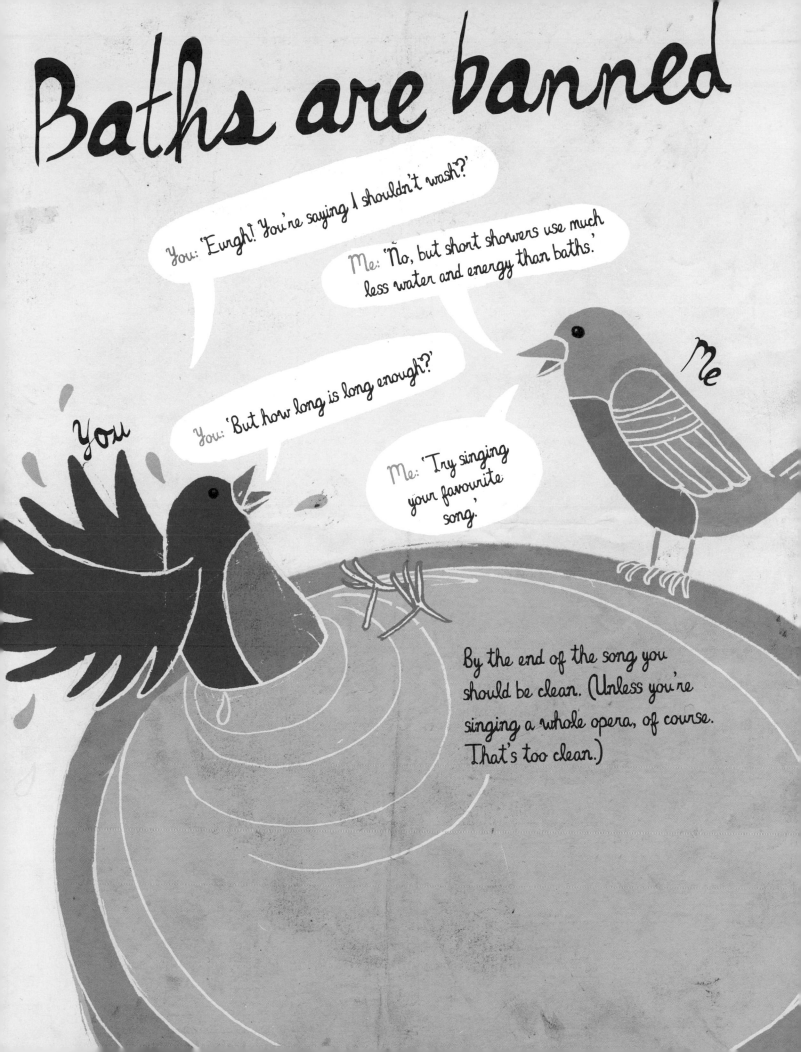

THE 'seriously, I'm TOO Grown Up For This NOW' SALE

Do you have tiny trainers, discarded dolls or babyish books hanging around and tripping you up?

Have a sale and raise some cash for something you care about.

If you have friends and family who also have stuff they don't need, have a GINORMOUS sale.

Pick a favourite charity and send them a letter explaining how you raised the cash - they'll love it!

THE GALLERY OF GOOD CAUSES

Set friends and family a challenge: everyone has one week to create a picture that represents their favourite good cause. They can use any medium of their choice (it could be painted, drawn, a collage or photographic). Next, put on an exhibition to sell the pictures and invite everyone. Remind visitors that they could be buying the Mona Lisa of the 21st Century! Money raised could go to one or all of the causes.

BE A LOCAL STAR

Buy stuff from your local farmers, shops and market, and encourage your family and friends to do the same.

This is good because it costs loads of money and uses loads of fuel to import food and other stuff from miles away. Plus, this way you get to know your neighbours and help support local businesses.

IDEA
Why not make the farmers and shop keepers a 'thank you for all your hard work' card at holiday times?

Bee The Change

We don't want our bees to BUZZ OFF – we need them! But gardeners have noticed that bees are less healthy and abundant than in the past. Bees fertilize plants by transferring pollen and seeds from one flower to another. When the plant is fertilized, it can grow and produce food. Without bees to spread seeds, many plants would die off.

So plant bee-friendly plants in a garden, on your windowsill, or any patch of ground you can find! Flowers that bees like include lavender, foxgloves and geraniums.

BZzzzzz

Bees get sluggish in the early morning or late at night. Once the sun comes out they liven up and can fly away. My sisters are very similar!

FUN RAISING

Want to raise cash for a good cause? Have a 'please-pay-what-you-can' party. For this task, get a gang of friends together and each choose a role from this list:

★ **The Host Post:** responsible for making a list of people to invite (and collecting the cash!)
★ **Arty Farty:** in charge of designing the invites and the decoration of the party room
★ **DJ:** in charge of music, including 'guest requests', plus lining up a favourite tune from each of the gang
★ **Captain Yumyum:** must make sure there's loads of fab food (ask each guest to bring one thing to share)

Give your party a name to match your cause – like 'The Tiger Ball' or 'Disco for Diabetes'.

Grow Your Own

Grow your own veggies, herbs or salad from seed. Growing your own plants will reduce the amount of food being imported, which, in turn, helps to reduce pollution. And loads of things thrive in pots. You can easily plant lettuce, tomatoes and chillies.

Celebrate your green fingers with a tea party featuring all the stuff you've grown! And you can give seeds to all your guests so they can do the same!

IT'S A WRAP

On family birthdays and special occasions, our house is full to the rafters with gift wrapping that just gets thrown away. So I've started wrapping presents with recycled paper for less waste. Have a look for some old stuff no-one wants anymore, such as:

- Maps
- Magazines
- Newspapers
- Sheet music
- Posters
- Wallpaper (but not stuff that's still on your walls!)

Another great idea is to make your own ribbon by cutting strips of old pillowcases or clothes.

My friend Graham often causes mischief by disguising the shape of the gift so you'd never guess what it is…

LONG-LASTING GLASS

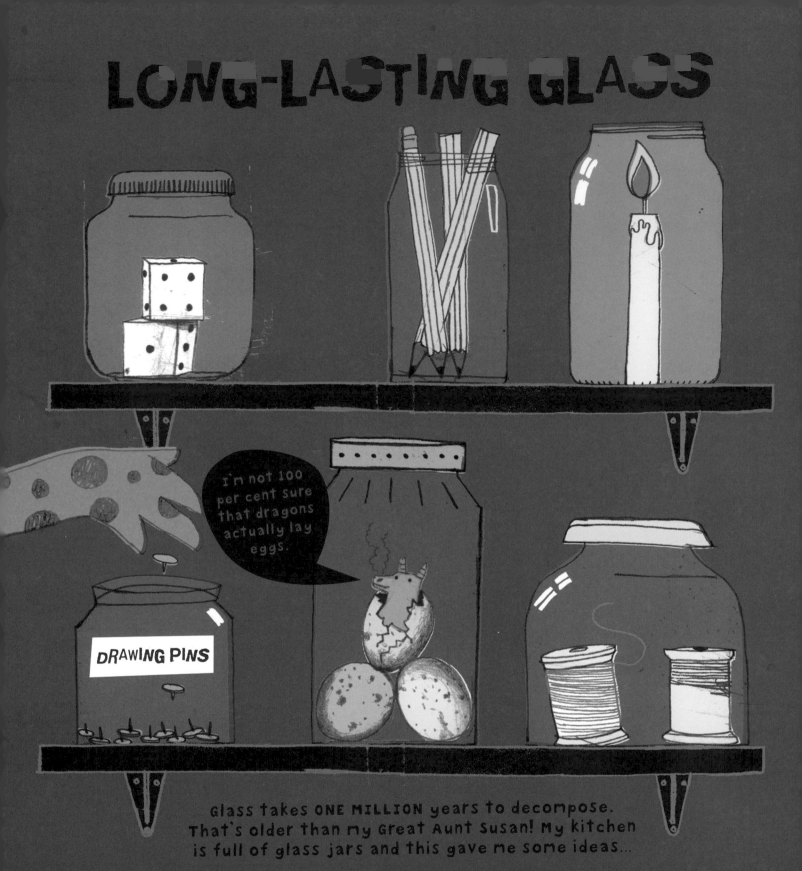

I'm not 100 per cent sure that dragons actually lay eggs.

DRAWING PINS

Glass takes **ONE MILLION** years to decompose. That's older than my Great Aunt Susan! My kitchen is full of glass jars and this gave me some ideas...

• Create a personalized gift for a friend by decorating a glass jar with his or her name. Use paint made especially for glass. You can make it even prettier if you tie a ribbon around the rim of the jar.

• You can always reuse old jars for storage. Make some cool handwritten labels, such as 'drawing pins' or 'dragons' eggs'.

Read All About It!

Make your own newspaper! Newspapers can be a bit gloomy, but yours could be full of ideas to help change the world for the better, and can include interviews, stories and pictures.

Pick a name for your newspaper like 'Fun News Doesn't Snooze' or 'Happy Times'. If you get an adult to photocopy your newspaper you could sell it to your family and friends and use the money raised for your favourite charity.

Veg Out

Did you know that cattle produce greenhouse gases that contribute to climate change? BUT there's a yummy way to combat this - eat less meat and more delicious veggies!

Vegetable Chilli

SERVES 6

- 1 grown-up, to help
- 1 tablespoon olive oil
- 1 onion, chopped
- 2 garlic cloves, finely chopped
- 1 green pepper, chopped
- 700g cooked beans (pinto, kidney or cannellini)
- 400g can crushed tomatoes
- 250g cooked corn kernels
- 1 chilli, deseeded and finely chopped
- 1 teaspoon dried oregano
- 3 teaspoons chilli powder
- 1 teaspoon ground cumin
- A pinch of salt

Method

1. With the grown-up's help, heat
the oil in a large pot.
2. Add the onion and sauté over a
medium heat until the onion is golden.
3. Add the remaining ingredients and
simmer gently, covered, for
30 minutes, stirring occasionally.
4. If it seems too thick, add
125ml of water at a time,
until it's just the way you like it.

Serve in bowls.

Plastic is NOT Fantastic

Enough plastic is thrown away each year to circle the earth FOUR times!

Here are three things you and your grown-ups can do to help:

❶ Carry a reusable water bottle.
❷ Carry a cloth bag for shopping.
❸ Go digital! No need for plastic DVDs when you can download films.

Why is Plastic Rubbish?

✳ It takes hundreds of years to decompose.
✳ Our oceans are filling up with it.
✳ Birds mistake it for food and it makes them sick!
✳ It can leak bad chemicals into the atmosphere.

Growing Up Together

Plant a tree! Why? Because trees provide habitat and food for wildlife, create oxygen for the atmosphere, feed the soil, look nice and are fun to climb!

You can plant one in your garden or even in a park, if you get permission. Take a photo on the same day every year of you and your friends beside the tree. See how much we all grow!

REMEMBER
You can grow trees from seeds (acorns or chestnuts) so you don't need to spend any money!

NIFTY THRIFTY

Donate your clothes to a charity shop
so someone else can use them. Then you can
buy something someone else doesn't need
anymore. Loads of stuff gets out-grown but
still looks like new. Plus, buying second-hand
is cheaper so there could be money left over
for fun activities like swimming or space travel.
(OK, maybe not quite enough for that last one.)
Other places you can get super second-hand
stuff from are garage sales, car-boot sales
or online marketplaces.

MAGIC IN THE MUD

Next to my house was a patch of muddy brown yuckiness filled with rubbish. We tidied all the rubbish away and sprinkled wild flower seeds over the ground. Hey presto! A few weeks later that ugly patch was beautiful and filled with colour. (The fun part was overhearing people talking about it. We do it everywhere now!)

And the flowers create a haven for bees, butterflies and other wildlife.

With an adult helper, try this in your neighbourhood. Don't forget to ask for permission first!

Boys Like Baking & Girls Like Dinosaurs!

Some people think boys and girls only like certain things. For example, boys like cars and girls like cooking, but I don't think that's true!

Gather two groups with equal numbers of boys and girls. Each group writes a list of their top ten favourite things in the world, then reads the list out to each other. I guarantee there will be some surprises – in my group half of the boys liked baking and all the girls wanted a pet dinosaur.

This may not sound like a world-changing exercise, but changing how people think really does make a difference!

SUPER

HELP! The world needs you to turn it into a nicer place! For this mission, you will need some willing friends/relatives.

1 Help each other invent superhero names, like Captain Hugtastic (good at hugging) or Trashgirl (great at clearing up rubbish) and then a name for the group like 'The Superkids League'.

HEROES

2 Decide on all the things your group would like to do to make the world a better place. Then work out who does what. (Captain Hugtastic could cheer people up with hugs.)

3 Make some superhero capes using old towels or blankets, and a mask for everyone. Anytime you need inspiration, gather your friends for a meeting, and wear your capes!

THE TOYS ARE REVOLTING!

Make mini placards from recycled card and lolly sticks and create a mini-protest with your toys to highlight issues you care about. The placards could say stuff like:

DRIVE LESS

WALK MORE!

This protest could go on display in a windowsill
or on a table so people can see it and be inspired.

FLYING YOUR FLAG

Design a beautiful flag out of a recycled sheet or pillowcase. You'll need acrylic paints or permanent markers. Write something inspirational on your flag like 'Let's Make Our World Even Better Together'.

Look at other flags and think about what colours and designs would work for your message.

Hang your flag where people can see it. On your window or on a pole in your garden would be great places.

TRASHTASTIC

Loads of rubbish just goes into landfill, but my Auntie Carol makes amazing sculptures out of all sorts of materials. Maybe you could get arty and make something amazing and beautiful out of it, too?

Your challenge is to create a sculpture out of rubbish for display at home, and make a sign for it explaining what it is.

If you do it with some neighbours, you could even have a rubbish exhibition.

Look out for things like card, plastic, foil and paper.

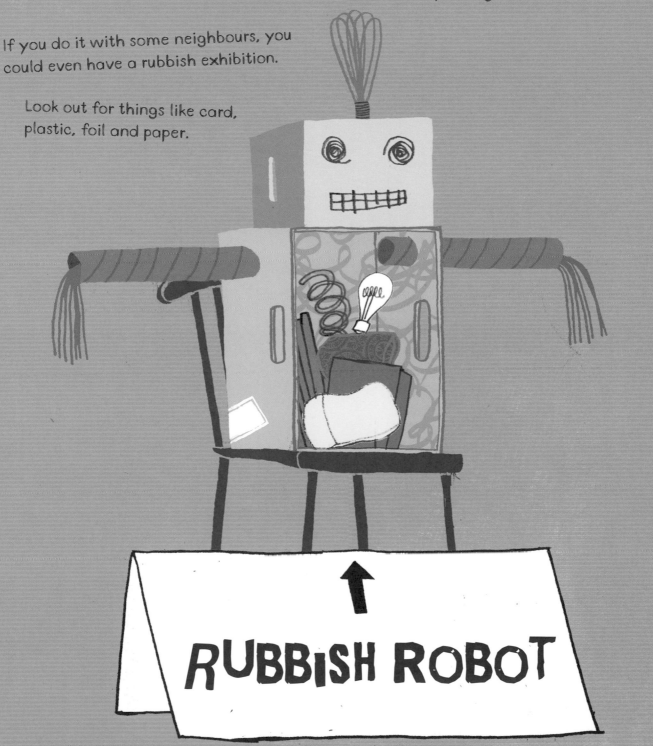

RUBBISH ROBOT

RADIO DAYS

In the olden days if you wanted to share your ideas, you had to write a letter and send it by horse and it'd take weeks to arrive. Now you can just record your own radio show! Interview your friends about stuff you've been doing to change the world, and experiment with fun sound effects (try dried peas for rain or coconut shells for hooves).

Borrow an adult's mobile phone to record yourselves, then email it or invite friends round to listen. Everyone hearing about your mission will be inspired!

NEWSFLASH

Make a TV out of an old cardboard box. Write and rehearse a pretend news show with a few stories.

Some examples could be 'Local charity shop is looking for donations' or 'Rainforests need our help'.

Find a name for your station like 'Channel Change'. Then broadcast your show live to friends and family from inside the cardboard TV, and maybe film it (borrowing an adult's mobile phone) and share the video with them.

The World is a Rainbow

I love that there are so many different people in the world. I have Nigerian, Irish, Turkish, Indian and Russian neighbours, which I think we should celebrate!

Draw around your hand, then colour it in any colour that you like. Ask your friends and family to join in and start to make a rainbow of the hands. Place it in a window where everyone can see it to remind them that we are all people, no matter what colour we are.

The Happiness Diary

Some people get sad more easily than others, but thinking positively can help. Even if you don't get sad that much, being positive is always a good thing! So write down three things every day in a happy diary:

1. Something I thought was beautiful.
2. Something that made me happy.
3. Something I am thankful for.

After a week, read it through. If you like it, carry on. It's a good habit to get into. Not a bad habit like biting your toenails. Not that I do that ... much.

A Beautiful World

If people notice what is beautiful about the world, I think they are more likely to want to look after it. So write a list of what is beautiful – it could rhyme but it doesn't have to. This is actually a really cool way of writing a poem. When you've finished you can keep it somewhere for inspiration, or read it aloud to your family and friends, or copy it and give it to someone (especially if they feel sad).

Here's mine:

I like seeing shapes in the clouds in the sky
I like eating apple and strawberry pie
I like walking my dog for miles and miles
I like my sister's gappy smile
I like the sun and I like the rain
I like visiting my mum at the seaside by train
Life is wonderful!

HEROES

We've already talked about superheroes - they are obviously cool. But there are everyday heroes in our lives who are just as important because they give us someone to look up to and make the world a better place. They just wear regular clothes though and don't get the attention. So think about who in your life is your hero and then write down why. Then tell them! They will be happy to be appreciated and you'll have the bonus of making a great person smile.

My hero is my mum who is funny and kind every day.

COMIC CAPERS

Create your own 'Be The Change' comic. Write a simple story about a super way of changing the world for the better in a maximum of nine sentences. Divide a page into squares to match the number of sentences, then tell your story with pictures plus word and thought bubbles. (Check out some comics to see how it's done.) You could sell your finished comic as a fundraiser for your favourite charity. Kapow!

STORY Bunting

Use bunting to tell everyone about 'Be the change'! Get some blank postcards, pegs, string, pens and crafty stuff for decorating. Carefully write out B-E-T-H-E-C-H-A-N-G-E, putting one letter on each postcard. On the other side, write something you've done to 'make it happen', then go wild decorating until it's the Greatest Bunting Ever (you can do it!). Peg the letters to string and display where it can be admired on both sides!

Rope in some friends to help. You could do it yourself but it might take a month and your hand would get tired from so much writing.

HOME CINEMA

Organize a film night. Sell tickets plus popcorn, sweets and ice cream. Invite as many people as you can fit in your house, being careful not to squash any small visitors. All funds raised could go to charity. You could try and match the film with the charity in some way. Why not start a regular film club once a month to raise money for a good cause?

The speaking spoon

Get a wooden spoon. Everyone gets to choose something they want to debate for up to two minutes. When they hold the 'speaking spoon' nobody can interrupt them until they've finished. Afterwards, they hand the spoon to anyone who has a question, but only the person holding the spoon can talk. The speaking spoon is a good way of resolving arguments.

Gandhi (who was from India and extremely wise) said:

'Be the change you wish to see in the world.'

It is super-good advice. Loads of wise people have said clever stuff over the years but I keep forgetting it. So I made a 'Little Book Of Wise Stuff' and every time someone says something good/ clever/inspiring I write it in there. I look in it if I am feeling a bit lost or confused. Why not start one for yourself?

My little book
of wise stuff

Other examples of wise words:

'Think happy, be happy.'
Anon

'No act of kindness is ever wasted.'
Aesop

'Most problems are solved with ice cream and a hug.'
My sister

THEY CAME FROM OUTER SPACE

WITH A BUNCH OF FRIENDS, MAKE A LITTLE SHOW PRETENDING TO BE AN ALIEN FROM ANOTHER PLANET, VISITING EARTH FOR THE FIRST TIME AND NOTICING ALL THE AMAZING THINGS ABOUT IT. PRACTISE, THEN PERFORM YOUR SHOW, WITH FACE PAINT AND WACKY ALIEN COSTUMES, REMINDING YOUR AUDIENCE HOW AMAZING THE WORLD IS AND HOW THEY SHOULD LOOK AFTER IT.

The Pledge

Get adults and kids in your neighbourhood to take the 'Be The Change' pledge. Write on a piece of paper: 'We promise to do everything we can to make the world a better place'. Ask people to sign underneath. Get everyone to write one thing that they will do that week next to their name. You can give them suggestions, too.

Walk instead of drive, plant a tree, think positive thoughts...

You get the idea!

Wishes for The World

Collect some twigs and arrange them in a vase. On luggage labels, write what you wish for the world. For example, 'I wish everyone had enough to eat' or 'I wish no one was cruel to animals', then tie them onto the twigs. Make a sign saying: 'This is our Wish Tree, with all the things we wish for the world. Please add yours.' Place it somewhere people might see it, like an after-school club or community centre.

My friend Tony, his son and their dog 'Silly Dog' are always eating fruit (they are a very healthy family), so when they're out walking they plant the seeds from the fruit wherever they are. You might think they wouldn't grow, but Tony says they've seen two apple trees as a result of their walk-planting. Whenever you have seeds or stones left over from fruit like plums, peaches or apples, get planting! Go back in a year and see what has happened.

An Apple a Day

Check with a grown-up first that it is ok to plant the seed in the place you have chosen.

The Society of Silliness

Seriously now, silliness is EXTREMELY important. Get your whole family to be silly for the day. Everyone must do a silly walk, a silly voice, a silly song, and then finish it up with a silly party where you have to do a silly dance to a selection of silly songs chosen by all.

This whole thing may seem, ahem, silly, but I guarantee there'd be much less arguing in the world if everyone took more time to be silly.

crazy cat

Silly=Happy!

Love
CAN CHANGE THE WORLD

If you love someone, then make sure you
tell him or her. It's easy to forget to do this,
and they will be very pleased if you do.

TIPS FOR THE SHY AND BASHFUL
Ok, so actually saying it might be embarrassing, or maybe
you don't see them that much. So instead, draw a heart and
send it to them or leave it somewhere they'll find it.

SAY SOMETHING NICE

Don't get caught up in saying mean stuff about people - everyone has something good about him or her. Sometimes mean or grumpy people are the ones most in need of a kind word. Next time you find yourself annoyed with someone, think of something nice to say to them - congratulate them on something they're good at ('your drawings are awesome!') or give them a compliment ('great jacket!').

NICENESS CAN CHANGE THE WORLD.

GREAT JACKET!

MY PERFECT WORLD

I think our imaginations are the most powerful tool we have to create change. So write down your idea of a perfect world and explain how you would fix all the things you think are wrong!

Then read it out to your family and friends, or at school or a club. You don't need to learn it, just make sure you've practised reading it out. You'll get people thinking about their own ideas!

(My sister said in hers there'd be chocolate growing on trees...)

Fashion Show

Use your creative talents and organize a fashion show. Choose recycled clothes and fabrics and invite everyone you know to see your gorgeous designs. You can charge an entry fee or sell the clothes to raise some funds. For inspiration, look at catwalk pictures - some of them are pretty wild, so you can go for it! And check out the way the models walk. Very snazzy. Practise your walk and strut your stuff.

HATS THE WAY TO DO IT

Sometimes people temporarily lose their hair when they are being treated for cancer — they can feel shy about it, plus get chilly when it's cold!

Ask everyone you know to donate hats, for kids and adults, and take your collection to a local hospital.

Make a 'feel better soon' card for the whole ward. Ask everyone who donates to sign it.

PHOTO-INSPIRATION ALBUM

Borrow a camera, and get some pens and card. Then ask friends to write a promise on the card, such as 'I'll walk to school every day'. Hold it in front of them and snap! Take as many pictures as possible, print them out for display and share them with your friends.

High five hello!

No one can resist a high five. If you see someone looking a bit sad, or bored, or lonely, even if you don't know him or her, offer a high five. If they don't know how to do one (like my friend Fred), you can teach them. Fred now high-fives with EVERYONE!

TIP: Go easy on the slap though. Not too hard.

Let It All Out !

Some people bottle up their anger and then it comes out in a burst. This is not good for peace in the world or people with sensitive ears. But it's ok to be angry sometimes – we all have those days. So you could do a 'controlled explosion'. With a friend or Mum and Dad, go somewhere you can have a big shout and let it out! You'll feel loads better. If other people see you, tell them what you were doing. In case they're scared.

WATER WORLD

These days there are more of us, but the same amount of water. So obviously saving water is a Good Thing. Try this: make fun speech bubble signs encouraging everyone to save water in lots of different ways, such as:

Above taps 'TURN ME OFF!'
On washing machines 'FILL ME UP!'
On leaky taps 'FIX ME!'
In your garden 'GIVE ME A WATER BUTT!'

The grown-ups will probably smile at this, and hopefully do something. You can keep an eye on them.

The Kids' Party

Kids must make their voices heard! You can't vote or make laws - but you can share your ideas and talk about what you think is right. Write a speech about what you would do if you were president/prime minister of the country. Include new laws you'd bring in, and changes you would bring about. Present your speech to the adults in your family (it might make them think).

Send your books around the world

Books are FANTASTIC - great for fun and for finding out all sorts of things. When you've grown out of yours, you can donate them to a charity shop. Write a message inside each book saying 'when you've read this, please pass it on' and sign it. Your book could get passed around the world...

Or you can use an organized project to send your books overseas for people who wouldn't ordinarily be able to get hold of books. Have a look online to find out about the various projects that run this service.

when life gives you lemons...

...make lemonade! A lemonade stand outside your house is a fantabulous way to raise money for your favourite cause.

RECIPE
1 grown-up, to help
9-10 large lemons
2 litres water
500g caster sugar

1. SQUEEZE the lemons until you have about ½ litre of juice. 2. In a separate container, SHAKE ¾ litre of the water and all the sugar together - but be sure to put a lid on your container first! 3. When the water looks clear, add the lemon juice to the mixture through a strainer. 4. Add the rest of the water and pop your lemonade in the fridge. YUM! Then cover a table in a bright cloth for your stand and make a sign saying: 'When life gives you lemons - make lemonade. Or buy ours!'

The OLD Ones Are The BEST

There's a lot to be learned from older people. They've been around longer and can know a lot more than younger people.

There are loads of good ways you can help them through volunteering, but the best of all is taking time to listen. They always have good stories. You can learn a lot of cool stuff from seniors that you wouldn't find in a book. Don't be afraid to ask.

KIDS ARE HEROES

Be inspired by other kids!

You might ask: 'What can I do? I'm just a kid.' I say: 'Anything!' Here are some hero kids from around the world. There's a space in there waiting for you.

Brandon Keefe,
collecting
books for
children's homes

Olivia Taylor,
raising funds
and awareness
for the
environment

Malala Yousafzai,
campaigning for
education rights

YOU!

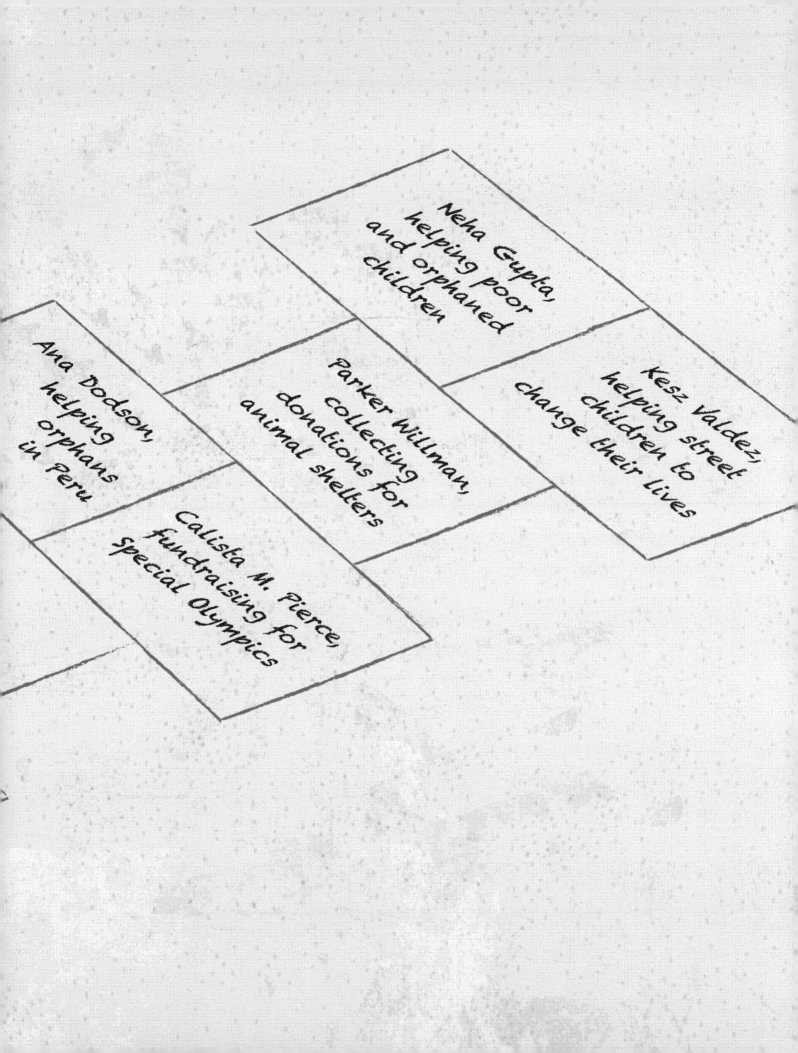

Hello neighbour

A wonderful way of making the world a better place is simple: getting to know each other better and being friendlier. So here's an idea. Make postcards for ten people on your street who you don't know very well. Draw pictures on the postcard of your family and write something like: 'Hello, we are your neighbours from 36a. We hope that you like living in this street. We hope to see you soon. If you see us, please wave.' I bet that'll work.

MY HOME HAS GOT TALENT

Let everyone show off their voices or musical skills and raise money at the same time: put on a concert at home. You can go solo with a backing track, recite your favourite piece of piano/kazoo/tuba music or perform a song with your friends. Make sure to charge for entry and most importantly: clap and cheer everyone so they all feel wonderful! It's a win-win situation!

THANK YOU DAY

Create your own 'Thank You Day'.

You could say 'Thanks mum for being patient with me when I nearly make us late' or 'Thank you for being my friend because it makes me happy'.

It's free to say thank you and makes people feel warm and fuzzy. Encourage others to join you, then everywhere you go you'll hear everyone saying 'THANK YOU' and see them smiling.

HANDS UP

Volunteering is great for helping people, making new friends and having fun. Stuff you can do includes: feeding animals at a shelter, visiting kids in hospital, being a reader for blind people, delivering food to seniors, clearing up in a wildlife reserve... decide what you'd like to do and ask a grown-up to help you investigate what's in your local area.

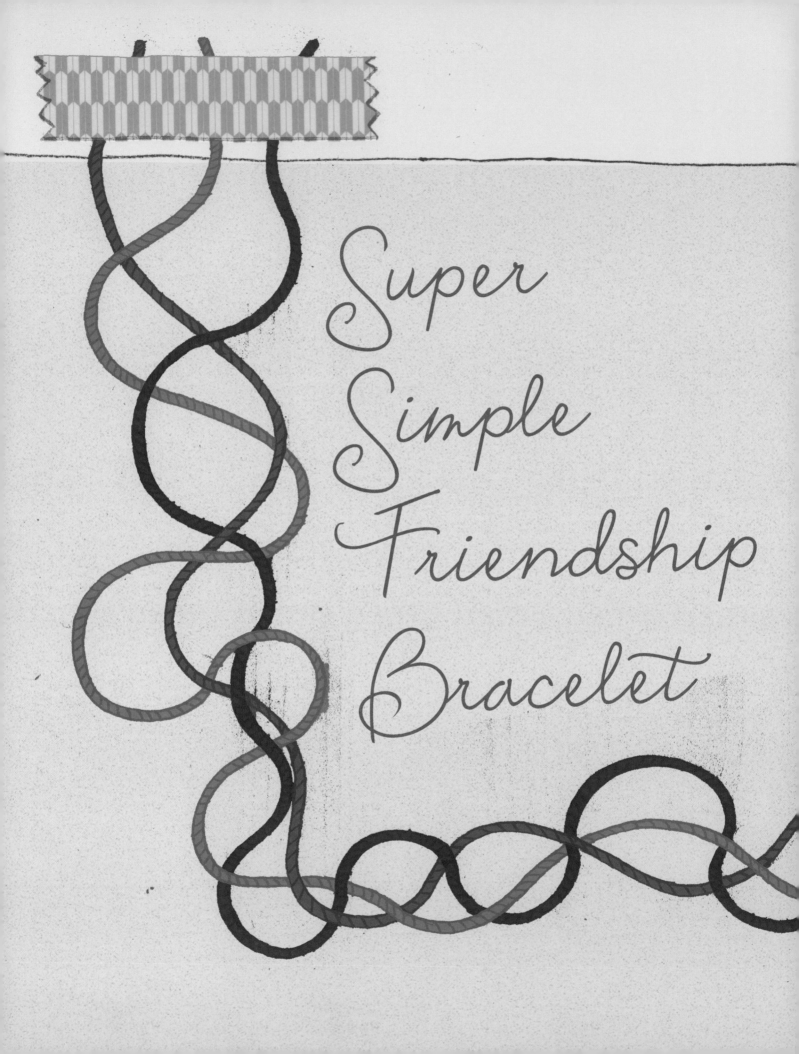

Super
Simple
Friendship
Bracelet

Your friends make the world a better place —so let them know they're special!

Get some wool in three great colours.

1 Cut three 25-cm lengths, one of each colour.

2 Knot them together at the top and tape the knot to a table to keep it steady. Fan out the three strands.

3 Get plaiting! Fold the left thread over the centre thread, then the right thread over the centre thread and then repeat, until you have a neatly plaited multicoloured bracelet.

4 Knot it at the end and cut off any straggly ends. It's now ready. Your friend can wear it around their wrist however they like.

Sweet Calculations

First: wash out a jar, the biggest one you can find.
Next, fill it with yummy sweets, counting them as you
put them in. Then, challenge your friends to guess the
quantity in the jar and charge them for each guess.
The nearest guess after, say, 20 guesses is the winner
of the jar, and they get to choose which good cause
the money goes to.

Telling Tales

TVs and computers are fun, but sometimes they can turn us into a load of mumbling zombies. For once, switch off the TV and put all electronic devices away. Gather the whole family, then try telling a story, one person saying one sentence at a time. Spending time doing something together is fun, plus it could turn out to be the Best Story Of All Time.

'Be The Change'
AWARDS

Hold your own awards ceremony - you could
make a red carpet out of a roll of red paper and
some statues out of cardboard sprayed gold.

Categories could include:
* Person who was kindest to animals
* Person who did most for kids
* Person who did the most recycling

Invite your friends and family or, if
you get permission, hold it at school.

WITH ONE FOOTSTEP...

Walking instead of driving is good for your health and for the planet. Encourage your whole family to walk as much as possible. Each month, keep a record of how many miles you have each walked and add it all together. If it's a larger number than the previous month, award yourselves a prize!

(Maybe ice cream. Then you could walk it off.)

Love your Librarian

Books can change the world. They teach us, make us laugh and inspire us. Librarians look after our books and make sure we have access to them for free, which is amazing.

Make your librarian a little homemade book, telling them why you love the library and what books you enjoy most. Not all heroes leap over buildings, remember. Librarians are quiet heroes.

Never forget the quiet heroes!

Going, going, GONE!

ORGANIZE A FUNDRAISING AUCTION.

1. Collect donations like toys or other things people no longer want.
2. Invite friends and family with a list of all the great stuff on offer.
3. Hold your auction.

The auctioneer should say:
'This cake starts at £1, do I have £2? Good, do I have £3?'
When no one wants to bid higher, they say 'going, going, gone – to Suzy Sponge* for £10'.

* Or whoever...

Good Gifts

Next time you have
a birthday party,
ask your guests to bring
a small gift to donate to a
children's hospital. You can
also do this at Christmas. Invite
everyone to wrap an extra present
to donate to shelters, care homes or
children's homes. Be sure to make a tag
for the present saying 'Happy Birthday/
Christmas/Easter, love from (your name).'

PRESENTS for PETS

Animal shelters always need extra food. You can help by asking your friends and neighbours - especially people you know who are pet owners - to donate a tin of pet food.

Other ways you can assist shelters is by helping to walk the dogs or fostering animals before they find their forever homes. Find out what your local shelter needs.

In their SHOES...

A VERY CHALLENGING THING FOR HOMELESS PEOPLE IS HAVING BAD SHOES. WET AND PAINFUL FEET ARE VERY DIFFICULT IF YOU SPEND MOST OF YOUR TIME OUTSIDE. COLLECT SHOES IN GOOD CONDITION FOR HOMELESS PEOPLE: BIG GROWN-UP SIZES ARE BEST. FIND OUT WHERE YOUR LOCAL HOSTELS AND SHELTERS ARE AND DELIVER THEM THERE. YOU WILL HAVE MADE SOMEONE'S LIFE MUCH EASIER...

The Story of YOU

Read your friend/family member a story in bed, but surprise them by replacing one of the character names with their name, to make them feel special. You could write a story especially for them. Everyone loves being read to - you could even offer to read stories to kids in hospital, or to your parents to repay them for reading to you.

Go Green!

Get an old t-shirt, and with a thick pen write eco-tips like:

1. Switch off taps
2. Turn off lights
3. Use less plastic
4. Walk, don't drive

Then, using face paint, give yourself a green face. People will definitely ask you why you're green, then you can teach them all you've learned about how to be a friend to the environment.

LITTER LEGENDS

Litter is bad. It can hurt wild animals and birds, blow into traffic lanes and pollute the environment.

So, become a litter legend. Get together with some friends and see who can fill the most bags.

Try and identify somewhere that is really full of litter and see how many bags you can fill. When I went litter collecting with some friends, we left a sign nearby saying 'Keep it Tidy – Litter Legends Were Here!'

I'm Sorry

Sometimes I'm grouchy. That's ok, it's just being human (or maybe I've turned into a monster. Mmm).

If you've been mean/naughty/grumpy, or think you should say sorry, then say it. Make a habit of saying sorry and forgiving other people when they do something wrong. You'll feel better, and you'll be contributing to Peace In The World.

GOOD FOR YOU!

Kindness.

There's a saying 'No act of kindness, however small, is ever wasted'. I reckon that's true. Try to be kind as often as possible. Help people carry shopping bags. Help mum and dad with chores. Help your brother/sister with their homework. Be nice to everyone you meet. And be kind to yourself. Kindness can definitely change the world.

HAIR TODAY, GONE TOMORROW.

CHALLENGE A TEACHER/PARENT/YOUTH LEADER TO SHAVE FOR A GOOD CAUSE. YOU CAN CHARGE PEOPLE A FEE TO WATCH IT HAPPEN. WHERE I LIVE, ALMOST EVERYONE HAS A BEARD SO I ORGANIZED A 'BEARD-ATHON' AND TEN OF MY FRIENDS SHAVED THEIR BEARDS OFF FOR CHARITY.

PS THEY COULD ALSO SHAVE THEIR HAIR OFF, BUT REMEMBER TO BUY THEM A HAT. THEY'LL GET CHILLY.

ODD BOD'S ODD JOBS

Offer to do chores for people who might need it, for free.
Write down the stuff you'll do on a menu like this:

- Washing-up
- Raking leaves
- Feeding their cat while they're away

To make it more fun, I dress-up when I do the odd job.
It livens up washing-up no end!

BACKYARD COMPOST

Composting is good because it reduces waste in landfills and improves the soil for our plants.

❶ Pick a spot away from direct sunlight.

❷ Turn a plastic bin upside down and cut out a lid.

❸ Add 1 part nitrogen (grass, coffee grounds/tea bags, fruit/veg scraps) to 3 parts carbon (leaves, straw, cardboard).

❹ It should be damp (not wet). Leave uncovered on a rainy day if it dries out.

❺ Give it a turn now and then in the summer.

❻ When it looks like soil, dig it into your garden and let the plants enjoy!

TREASURE CHEST

Put some 'treasure' (drawings, books, etc) in an old box and hide it. Then create a treasure hunt for your friends. Draw a map and leave clues, such as sticky notes saying 'nearly there' or chalk arrows on the pavements.

Everyone who plays has to donate something they don't use anymore, like an old toy, which you can give to charity afterwards.

FUNNY FACE COMPETITION

This competition
comes in two rounds.
Everyone makes a small donation
to enter. First, the kids judge the adults
and decide who can make the silliest face.
Then the adults judge the kids. When there's
a kid and a grown-up winner, they have
to compete for 'overall winner'.
The money can go to your favourite
good cause. Remember
to take photos!

Recycled Greetings

Make greeting cards for
friends and family out of
recycled materials. Get your
parents to save cardboard
boxes, magazines, fabric
and other stuff you could
use to make beautiful cards.

Here's one I made for my mum
with buttons for eyes, string
for a mouth, words cut out
of an old magazine saying
M-U-M, all glued onto card
from an old shoe box and
coloured in.

The
BEST
Things in Life
ARE FREE

Draw some bank notes with a picture of you on them, but instead of writing '1 pound' on them, write '1 favour'. Give these to friends and family as gifts. When they hand their notes over you have to do one favour for them, such as clean their bike. So it's basically a gift token but it doesn't cost you any real money. Brilliant!

MY TOP

10

MAKE A LIST OF THE TOP TEN CAUSES OR
CHARITIES THAT ARE IMPORTANT TO YOU.

THINK ABOUT WHICH ACTIVITY YOU COULD
DO TO HELP OR RAISE MONEY FOR EACH OF
YOUR TOP TEN CAUSES.

KEEP A RECORD OF WHAT YOU DO, AND
WHEN YOU HAVE DONE SOMETHING FOR EACH
ONE, GIVE YOURSELF A MASSIVE CHEER! (PLUS
REMEMBER TO DO A CELEBRATORY DANCE.)

Websites

To donate your books to other kids who need them:
Books For Africa
www.booksforafrica.org

International Books Project
www.intlbookproject.org

Little Free Library
www.littlefreelibrary.org

To find out about amazing stuff that other kids have done:
Kids Are Heroes
www.kidsareheroes.org

To learn more about nature and how you can help the earth:
Earth Kids Kids Club
www.earthskids.com/kidsclub.aspx

To find out more about ecological issues:
Eco Friendly kids
www.ecofriendlykids.co.uk

To help other kids get the opportunities they deserve:
Kids Change The World
www.kidschangetheworld.org

To find out where you can find cool kid's clothes from brands that are Fairtrade, organic, or recycled:
Style With Heart
www.stylewithheart.com/category/kids

To find out about your rights as a kid and how to stand up for the rights of your fellow kids:
Save The Children
www.savethechildren.org.uk
Enter search for Funsheets

To find out how to grow veggies, plant a bee-friendly garden and get green fingers:
Kids In The Garden
www.kidsinthegarden.co.uk

To find out more about recycling:
Recycling
www.benefits-ofrecycling.com/recyclingforkids

To find out more about bullying and how you can stop it:
Stop Bullying
www.stopbullying.gov

To find more ways to help our animal friends:
Peta Kids
www.petakids.com

To read about other inspirational kids who have Changed The World, and to see how you could nominate someone for the Peace Prize:
Children's Peace Prize
www.childrenspeaceprize.org

Although every endeavour has been made by the publisher to ensure that all content from these websites is age appropriate, we strongly advise that Internet access is supervised by a responsible adult.